I Listened For His Breath

I Listened For His Breath

Nancy Seriani

ReadersMagnet, LLC

I Listened For His Breath
Copyright © 2018 by Nancy Seriani

Published in the United States of America
ISBN Paperback: 978-1-948864-64-0
ISBN Hardback: 978-1-948864-65-7
ISBN eBook: 978-1-948864-66-4

All rights reserved. No part of this publication may be reproduced, stored in a retrieval system or transmitted in any way by any means, electronic, mechanical, photocopy, recording or otherwise without the prior permission of the author except as provided by USA copyright law.

The opinions expressed by the author are not necessarily those of ReadersMagnet, LLC.

ReadersMagnet, LLC
10620 Treena Street, Suite 230 | San Diego, California, 92131 USA
1.619. 354. 2643 | www.readersmagnet.com

Book design copyright © 2018 by ReadersMagnet, LLC. All rights reserved.
Cover design by Ericka Walker
Interior design by Shieldon Watson

Contents

Chapter 1	Magic On The Desert Floor	7
Chapter 2	Waltzing In The Rockies	15
Chapter 3	Pink vs. Blue	23
Chapter 4	Hobby Farming and Kids	27
Chapter 5	Memorial Day 1987	33
Chapter 6	The Little Red Schoolhouse	35
Chapter 7	The Diagnoses	43
Chapter 8	Fulfilling Sacraments	55

Chapter 1

Magic On The Desert Floor

He was amazed, angered, and sarcastic upon meeting the young woman who would eventually one day become his bride.

George was old schooled, being a son of Italian immigrants who had found their way to the south side of Chicago in the early 1900s. Born in 1938, George was the youngest of four children until ten years later when his twin sisters were born.

His father and brother were cement masons and even as a young child, George went along on jobs with them. He was never too interested in school or homework. His main interest was becoming a cement mason.

At sixteen years of age, he left Chicago and moved to Phoenix where he could work year round doing what he loved most—finishing concrete.

That was back in the day when labor unions were only starting to become really united and he found out quickly there was a huge difference in skilled labor and union rules from one state to another. Arizona was a "right-to-work" state. Union labor in any trade was not real popular in those days for anyone other than union members.

He had come from a union strong hold in Illinois, but found a different story in Arizona. He had learned much from family and friends before moving west and intended to share that knowledge any way he could to help his union brothers succeed. He had nothing to lose and everything to gain.

George quickly found his place among his union brothers and became instrumental in organizing a solid foundation for which members could be proud. All of that took many years with a lot of hard work, determination, fighting, drinking and meetings. Oh yes, and did I mention fighting and drinking?

Arizona was not union friendly back then, so any new changes came with much trial and tribulation. Construction, labor trades, fighting, and drinking all went hand in hand. It's the way it was. They worked hard and for lack of better words, played hard. Eventually the cement mason's union became stronger: membership grew and yet changes were still on the way.

George became an icon within his local union. He mastered his trade and taught others the art of concrete.

However, in early October 1979 at six o'clock one morning, he got to the job that would change his life forever. Everything had seemed so normal to him that day. Hung over from the night before and four concrete trucks sitting backed up spinning and ready to be dumped out. The concrete foreman and finishers gathered together discussing their plan for the day. Nothing out of the ordinary to him, but there, standing next to the boss was a woman being introduced to the men as the new apprentice.

I was a lot of things that morning. Scared, nervous, and tired from not sleeping the night before in anticipation. After the boss introduced me to George, I had another feeling. The feeling was somewhere between humiliation and intimidation. George asked me if I was lost—shouldn't I be barefoot in my kitchen chasing kids and baking chocolate chip cookies? I just stood there, pissed off and in shock. As he turned and walked away from me, I looked at the boss, started to laugh, and said "that guy has got no ass at all". George's butt was flat as a pancake and he used suspenders to hold up his jeans. The boss grinned and assured me that George had plenty of ass.

My first day on the job was at the very least overwhelming. Women were only just beginning to enter the building trades and at that time, I was one that felt I needed to prove to men that women could handle it and that we deserved to work for equal pay. Myself, I had just about had it with working my ass off in factories, right next to a man doing the same work (only slower) getting more money than me. What! That's enough! This is when I decided to join the building trades. Union labor with union representation. I decided to become a cement mason. Almost immediately after joining, I was working.

My first job lasted three weeks until we finished it. During those weeks to say I worked extremely hard would be an understatement. George was the machine man on the job and although he was not "the boss", he did run the job. Concrete is ready when the machine man says so. He constantly pointed to me for three weeks. He never spoke, only pointed. Each time he pointed it meant something.

The journeyman finishers were all, for the most part, very helpful in teaching me what to do, when to do it, and how to do it. There were two that were especially wonderful, Michael and Daniel. They too had been George's apprentices. Every day I felt like I'd done something wrong because George seemed so angry. I took it all so personal. The guys kept telling me they went through the same regiment and that George would be the one that would make me or break me.

Each day I would gain more confidence and just do better. My work ethics and morals were shining as I entered George's world. I was so self-conscious trying to fit in a man's world and yet so self-confident. Work did not scare me. The harder, more physical the work was, the more I succeeded. I was a Wisconsin farm girl and all I really knew was how to work hard.

The last day of my first job finishing concrete, George spoke to me. I was naturally on my hands and knees troweling the edges when he walked over and said, "Come on, I'll buy you lunch." I looked up and said the boss hadn't told me to go for lunch yet, but

George said it would be alright, he'd take care of it. Something made me get up off my knees and follow him.

We had been pouring a slab for a new department store inside a mall where other stores had already opened. One of which was a baked potato place. That's where we went. I was totally amazed by the whole thing. Any kind of topping for a baked potato that you could think of they offered. Plus, I was hanging out doing lunch with the main guy on the job, and he was even talking to me nicely. I didn't think life could get any better.

It was the first of many enjoyable lunches we would share. We finished the job that day. We were all given our checks and our lay-off slips. I was ecstatic and sad. My check was bigger than any check I'd ever seen with my name on, but I'd never seen a lay-off slip before. I guess I thought I was going to work there forever. All the guys shook my hand and said it had been a pleasure to work alongside me. Some said I worked harder than most men and others hoped if they had to work with other women, they'd all work as hard as I did. The truth was, as I'd find out later, there were women on jobs with the attitude that they really didn't have to work hard because the government made it a law that every job had to have a certain percentage of minorities working which included women. Those women did not make what I was trying to do any easier. All in all, it had been a fabulous three weeks. I had a pocket full of money, I had made some friends, and was headed back to the union hall to get my next job.

I was the first one there before the hall opened talking to the business agent. He'd already heard I'd done well and that I'd have another job before I left that day.

I waited patiently as men walked in, picked up their work orders, and passed by; some without even so much as a hello. Others nodded at me, and some introduced themselves. There seemed to be some commotion in the parking lot just outside the back door. Some of the guys I had spent the last three weeks working with had arrived at the hall drunk. George was one of them. Loud, obnoxious, and arrogant. I couldn't hardly believe it was the same guy. The business agent called me to the window and handed me a work order for the following day. I was relieved to have a job and couldn't wait to get away from the guys and their drunkenness.

Next day I went to a job on the other side of Phoenix and who was there? Most of the same guys I'd worked with on my first job. George was there too. He looked different than he did the night before at the hall. He sounded different. He seemed to be two different men. At least it seemed that way to me. As the weeks passed by and jobs were started and completed, I learned a huge amount about finishing concrete and a whole lot more about the man named George.

I had managed to excel at the job and also had gained the respect of the men I was spending so much time with. Every job I was meeting different finishers. Nearly every job I was on, George was on. Once the ice had broken over a baked potato, we became friends.

He had openly admitted and talked about his colorful past to me. Many others were anxious to tell me all about their opinions concerning George also. Some were more tactful than others. I was definitely being painted a picture of something and someone I'd not yet known of in my life. I was also not so sure I wanted or needed to know any more. Truth was though, there seemed to be a connection between this out of the ordinary man and this farm girl, hippy chick turned cement finisher.

Halloween evening proved to be a big turning point in each of our lives. Some of the guys were getting together at a bar near the union hall. I was considered one of the guys and had decided I'd meet them. By the time I got there most of them were already in the bag and there sat George at the end of the bar motioning for me to sit next to him.

He had a glass of something in front of him, but he wasn't being loud and crazy. I sat down alongside of him. He leaned over and said he had to get out of there, would I like to go for a drive. I wasn't much of a drinker and really didn't do the whole bar scene much. I agreed and we left with the usual snide remarks and innuendos from the guys bellied up to the bar.

We got into his car and started driving, talking, laughing and before long the lights of Phoenix were far behind us. You can find out a lot about a person on a road trip. The more George spoke, the more I wanted to know. He was the most interesting person I'd ever talked to. I clung to his every word. There were many things about him I questioned. I could hear things he wasn't saying. I could feel pain and hurt from him even as he made light of everything.

He was an alcoholic, twenty-five years strong and trying to quit. He had been drinking soda at the bar we had just left, hoping I would stop in. Up to this point, I hadn't even considered such a thing. I didn't do drunks and I had made that perfectly clear. Life was short and I had made up my mind as a youngster that I wouldn't spend my life hooked up with any man that would love a bottle more than me. It was just one of my rules.

And there, I sat in a car somewhere in the middle of the desert in Arizona falling for a beautiful Italian man with a real vivid past. A past I would continue to learn about for the next twenty-five years, one story after the other. Some pretty stories and some not so much. Being that as it may, we had many things in common.

From that night on, George and I became as one in everything we did. It all just seemed so right. He needed something I could offer and I wanted to know everything he knew. He seemed mystical but hard headed. He was balanced and yet wild. He appeared committed to family, friends, fishing and finishing concrete.

We sat on the desert floor under a full moon that night, staring into one another's eyes. Speaking no words, we talked through our hearts. It seemed electric around us as if we were glowing in the darkness. It was something from somewhere we had never been. We were mesmerized by each other's presence. It was soulful.

We were beginning to embark on a loving relationship with many obstacles in the way. Mostly the barriers consisted of others and their opinions. Whether it had to do with love, concrete or fishing, people had their minds made up. They were convinced that George was unworthy of a loving woman and would have no time or patience for a woman that would have to be taught everything about concrete and fishing. The biggest deal for them was George was fifteen years my senior and we seemed to be from two different planets, or at the very least from different generations.

Those were all issues for everyone but us, and was part of the beauty of our connection. He'd had his share of bar flies and I'd had my share of boys. Each of us were ready for something different and neither of us were willing to settle for anything less.

We became partners. We rented a studio apartment and quickly settled into a comfortable home like environment.

I met his family. His mother had been widowed for less than a year, but still Sundays were for family and pasta. It was a most wonderful Sunday afternoon that first time. George's teenage son, who lived there with his grandmother, was quiet most of the day. I took that to mean he was not fond of the idea that his dad was involved with me. I was wrong about that though. Turns out he was just not very fond of his dad.

After George's initial move to Arizona, in 1953, he traveled back to Chicago many times to visit family and friends and to work. He had met a woman there and in his mid twenties moved her to Phoenix where they were married. Six months later she delivered their son. One week later she passed away from complications of child birth. George crawled into a bottle of whiskey and stayed there for a long, long time. Meanwhile, George's parents took the infant son to raise at his request.

George so loved his wife and could not make sense of how and why she should die when so many whores walked the streets. Why would she not breathe and live and dance and raise a family when others, who in his eyes were unworthy, would enjoy all life's rewards.

He became bitter. The more bitter he became, the more he drank. The more he drank, the more bitter he was. Somewhere along the way, it just became easier for him to be mad.

He didn't have much to say about the way his folks were raising his son. If he disagreed about anything, it only caused family problems. If he showed discipline, it only caused more family problems so his solution was drink, work, give the kid money, and fish whenever he could. Every time he looked at his son, he was reminded of a life they never got to have. He knew only one thing for sure and that was that by allowing his folks to raise his son, he gave him the best life he could considering the sad circumstances.

And of course, we all know that even our best decisions made are often scrutinized by others. I have learned that unless your situation is even remotely the same, until you walk that line, you have no right to criticize.

I tried to help everyone make the best out of a not so good situation. But, try as you may sometimes, your best is just not good enough for some.

Chapter 2

Waltzing In The Rockies

GEORGE AND I HAD a carefree life. He taught me all things concrete. He taught me about the fine skill of fishing. Concrete and fishing became our lifestyle. Traveling to and from jobs and lakes was not limited only to Arizona. We had family all over the country who were also cement finishers and fishermen.

George and I had taken a job that was to be around the clock and out of town. It took hours to drive there, but the scenery through the state was awesome. A high security job site on the wing dams underneath Lake Powell. We worked all day and all night. Sometime in the wee hours of morning we finished and were given our checks. We got in the car and headed down the mountains for Phoenix.

I opened my check. I couldn't believe what I was seeing. George told me they had turned me out on that job. Turned out meant I had graduated from apprentice to journeyman. I had full pay and mileage on one big fat check. I couldn't hardly stand the excitement. He was so proud of me. It made for a lot of conversation on the ride home.

We drove straight to the union hall and each of us got work orders for the next day at the nuclear power plant. They said the job would last about a week, so without any hesitation, we drove home, got the fishing car, and went for the rest of the day to Lake Pleasant. Life was good.

We worked for the next week, twelve hours a day. At the end of the week, we got our checks, cashed them, loaded the car, and went to Colorado to visit the nephews.

It was early spring in Arizona, but still very wintery in Colorado. I'd never taken a road trip like that. The roads were clear, the sun was shining and the steep Rocky Mountains were covered in deep snow. We would get out of the car without jackets and dance in the snow. As far as you see in every direction was snow, lots of snow. The mountains were so vast and so breath taking. The whole trip was overwhelming. In the vastness of it all was just George and me, our road buddies, Willie Nelson, and Bob Seger and beauty indescribable. Love was everywhere.

After a fourteen hour drive, we arrived in the middle of the night. The family was thrilled to see us and before long it was daylight and time for everyone to go to work. George went with the nephews. He had been so proud of them starting their own company. They were the best cement finishers in town. And the nephews were just as proud to have "Uncle" on the job with them. They had been telling their laborers and the concrete truck drivers about "Uncle" for quite some time. That morning "Uncle" showed up on the job. Everybody jumped through hoops to impress the famous "Uncle". They were rewarded for their efforts throughout the day with pieces of candy. If the driver backed in and dumped out the way the shoot man wanted, he got a piece of candy. If the laborers mucked without complaint, they'd get a piece of candy. He was "Uncle", the candy man to each of them.

Once George and I had committed to each other, drinking was out of the picture. I started buying bags full of hard candies and he'd keep his pockets filled every day. It became his thing. Anyone who had ever known him in his drinking days were astounded at his sobriety, especially his nephews.

It gave them great pleasure to get to know the uncle who had changed from night to day. He was happy, peaceful, and positive. He seemed a new man to them. He was a new man in many ways.

The guys made a couple of more pours that week and then it was time for fishing. They took us high into the Granbys where, I believe, God lost his shoes. It was spectacular. It was cold, but oh so beautiful. We caught rainbow trout all day long. We picnicked and played and life was just so good.

We'd had a wonderful visit with the family and were anxious to get back to warm and sunny Arizona and our own work and fishing holes.

George and I talked and sang all the way home. He told me he was grateful to me for coming into his life. He felt that I was the one who changed him and allowed the better side of his life in. I told him it wasn't me.

The truth was, he changed himself. He was ready to quit drinking. He quit and got a life. That life was with me. If he hadn't quit, he would have still had a life, it just wouldn't have been with me. That's all. He did it, not me. Yes, there were many, many talks and yes there were many temptations. My answer was simple and always the same—you're a grown man capable of making decisions. Do what pleases you and what will make you proud of yourself the next day. I wasn't the judge. He had to be his own judge. If he couldn't please himself, he sure couldn't please me.

I trusted him to do right by himself. It took him a long time to believe in and trust himself the way I knew he could. He was the strongest man I'd known. His will power was phenomenal. It showed his strength of character. I admired him. Every now and then when we'd leave a party, he'd be so upset by his friends drunkenness and sloppiness because he knew in his day he'd been worse than any of them. The guilt and shame he felt for his actions served to strengthen him even more.

The more time passed, the more good he'd try to pack into a day. It was as if he were trying to make up time. Time spent in a bottle.

Wasted time. Wasted energy. A wasted life. He felt like God had given him another chance to get it right and he took it and ran.. This time he ran in the right direction.

Days were better than nights. He could mostly control what happened during the day time hours, but nights were different. He had dreadful nightmares. Many nights were treacherous. I learned to just lay low when he'd wake up swinging. His past haunted him. Day and night, he was constantly on guard. I never had known such things like being in a room with your back to the wall watching the door or walking through the front and exiting the back.

I just did what he asked. It was my innocence that kept me and him grounded. I never felt it was my place to question anything that had ever happened to him. If he felt I had a need to know, he'd tell me. Stories that others thought I should know had become an issue for a while until one day I not so politely told a couple of guys just what they could do with their stories. I couldn't have ever known who was telling the truth and who wasn't. Half the time George couldn't even remember the stories. Maybe he was there and in a blackout or maybe he wasn't even in the neighborhood. Some people felt this obligation to spill their guts to me, but meantime while they were, they were also drunk.

All I really cared about was that I was grateful for whatever, whenever, and whoever about George because if he hadn't been or done all things just as he did we would not have been. Because of this attitude nothing else mattered. My major concern was to just be happy. Keeping George happy, made me happy.

Life after one quits drinking, changes. Actually, it has to. George had been one of those drinkers that wouldn't let somebody sit at the bar without a drink in front of them. He was also one of those drinkers who for no reason at all was likely to knock your head off just because he felt like it. And if he did feel like it, more times than not it would be several people scrambling to pick themselves up off the floor, if they even could.

Part of me was attracted to that. You know how they say that girls like the bad boys. I'd never actually seen him fight but I felt safe knowing he could. Considering many of the tales that I'd been told, the attraction of the mysterious man increased. Our love just continued to grow. We asked nothing more than mutual respect for one another. That's what each of us got and much, much more. It did seem though that something was missing. Maybe not missing, just wasn't in the picture yet.

I'd had the honor of getting to know his Arizona family and friends and some in Colorado, even a few that had been on vacation from Chicago. They all thought I was better than sliced bread. They thought I had turned this animal into a peaceable man. I didn't think it then nor do I think it now. I believe when one gets totally ready to change their life, they do it. If they're successful, they never look back. That's what happened to George. Yes, OK, he found someone. Me. But that alone would not have been enough if he had not truly wanted something different for his life.

Saying you're going to quit any habit doesn't just make it go away. The willpower, the strength within you is what helps you or doesn't. He had to first commit to changing his old habits in order to commence starting new ones. I just became his new habit. Lucky for me. Lucky for George. Really lucky for both of our families. His family knew there needed to be a change for George. They seen him begin the change and continue on with it.

My family hadn't even met him. My brother and sister had come to Phoenix and stayed overnight, but George was in Chicago working at the time. That was shortly after we had gotten our apartment. They had rode from Wisconsin and were headed to Florida. There was some sort of mechanical problem with my brother's motorcycle. George had told me, on the phone, to take them to Michael's house. He said that Michael would probably grumble a bit since it wasn't a Harley Davidson, but he'd fix it. That's what happened alright. Grumbled a bit was an understatement. Brother followed behind me on his bike. I was driving the fishing car and pulled up at Michael's. There he stood on the sidewalk in front of his garage. Arms folded across his chest with a can of Bud in one fist, cement finishers' arms bulging from his black t-shirt and a cigarette hanging out of his growly face. His long yellow hair tied back.

Although Michael loved me, he questioned every man who rode anything other than a Harley. And now here I was asking him to allow this thing onto his driveway and into his garage and try to fix whatever it was so they could be on their way. He begrudgingly did fix the bike and even offered my brother a beer. I've always said, God works in mysterious ways. They all met again many years later and the day in Michael's garage became a very fond memory.

Other than myself, Michael was George's best friend. Their first meeting was at the union hall. Michael had just gotten out of the Navy. It was late 60s early 70s. Michael's mother was secretary for the union hall. She and George had worked together for years already by then and were wonderful friends. Michael became one of George's apprentices. He really became George's favorite. They had a lot in common. Work, drinking and fighting. And along comes Danny, another of George's apprentices. Michael and Danny loathed each other in a good way and they both loved George. He was, for sure, their mentor in every way. They were also fishing and hunting partners.

From all accounts and with different versions of each story, I'm not so sure if any of them had licenses for anything—fishing, hunting, or driving. What I am sure of is that, to have lived in the day, was to have really lived. Alright, so they lived right on the very edge. It was a simpler time. Life wasn't so rushed. Priorities were different so commitments were also different. Another thing I'm sure of is these men remained true to themselves and stood up for what they believed in. They were for sure a band of brothers. United by concrete, bonded by belief.

I fit right in. Mostly all of the guys loved me at first because of George. However, there were a handful of them that just couldn't bring themselves to accept me for any love nor money. I referred to them as "George's chauvinists friends". Pigs, if you will.

They'd run work-big jobs-call for George as machine man. If they didn't have room for an apprentice, they wouldn't be needing him. Some men had a real pissed off attitude about women in the building trades.

Some men would not have a woman on the job, including myself, no matter what. Most of these men had been George's friends for many years.

I would have just loved to have been able to really push the matter, cause a scene, posed as a threat. I, too, was from a union family. I also knew that I was one of only four female finishers in the state of Arizona. I wasn't going to have a lot of support. I settled for my own work ethic, served my apprenticeship like anybody else and just worked, played, and fished. I would eventually gain my own respect outside of being George's lady. And so it was. George just wouldn't take the job if they didn't want me too. That was all good with us. We'd either get another job or go fishing.

Chapter 3

Pink vs. Blue

George knew Lake Pleasant like the back of his hand, broken bones and all. George, Michael, and several others poured the first boat ramp there. George would stay on shore after the pour each day and fish all night. It remained his favorite job ever!

Lake Pleasant had become one of our favorite lakes in Arizona. For one reason, it was the closest to Phoenix. Many a day we'd pour concrete from 4 a.m. till noon and then head to the lake and fish till dark. Sometimes all night long. It was quiet. It was calm. It was healing. We would talk sometimes. Sometimes we wouldn't. Nature would speak and we listened. Fishing was not just about catching fish. It was about cleansing oneself. It was about just being. Gathering thoughts. Being able to think through those thoughts. Being able to freely discuss thoughts and feelings with each other without judgment. It was also about the money. Whoever caught the first fish, the biggest fish, and the most! The first fish caught, that was legal, paid a quarter. The biggest and most paid fifty cents each.

I had painted blue dots on George's quarters and pink dots on mine. Believe me, when he opened his tackle box, he had a lot of my pink quarters. Over time though, I learned a thing or two from him and really ended up many days with a good share of blue quarters in my box.

We'd also fish boat against boat with Michael and his wife, Susie. George had taught Michael about fishing. Michael had taught Susie. George had taught me. And one thing that Michael, Susie, and I could be sure of, was that George was the captain at all times. It seemed he was always in the know. Like he could see beneath the water and just know where to be. Bass did not have a chance when George was fishing. Nor did crappies or catfish.

All the Arizona lakes were wonderful. If we'd go during the week, it was like we were the only ones there. That was back in the day when we never even heard of jet skis. The lakes were for fishermen and families camping for a weekend. Hardly anyone ever went to Saguaro or Bartlett Lakes because of the washboard roads to get there. Apache Lake was gotten to by a switch back dirt road and Roosevelt and Alamo Lakes were a long distance from Phoenix. But we fished them all.

Many of the trips were overnighters. I had picked up a 1963 Plymouth for $300.00 in 1979 when I first got to Arizona. George and I turned that car into our fishing car. We bought a brand new 12 foot MirroCraft aluminum boat that he and I would slide up over the trunk of the car onto rails we had welded on the roof. We'd tie it down front and back and it wouldn't move. We had also bought a brand new, never been used, Honda 10hp outboard motor. We kept that in the trunk with our tackle boxes, poles, and net. We had taken the back seat out of the car and that's where we kept the coolers and sleeping bags. We'd also taken out the front bench seat and replaced it with two real fancy swivel bucket seats. The seats laid all the way back too. We had quite the motor home. Push button drive and all.

There's a story behind no back seat and replacing the front seat to swivel bucket seats in the fishing car. George and another finisher friend were on their way home from fishing Lake Pleasant as a storm was brewing. Crossing a simple little short dip, the road gave way under the blacktop. The front bumper of the car was hung up on the edge, unable to go anywhere. Down the wash coming right towards George was a rushing flash flood. It just rocked the car as the flood waters got deeper. The friend fled the car, but no, George was staying. His boat was on the top of his car. Captains go down with their ship. George wasn't moving. The car eventually stopped running. He stayed right there as the water filled the car up to his chest until help came. They finally got the car out of the wash and hauled over to Michael's. When they drained the transmission, it looked like pink pudding. The seats smelled like the inside of a chicken coop. And that's how the seats came to be.

So this was our life.

My sister, Amy, was getting married in June and a perfect opportunity to introduce all the family to him. There was no long lengthy planning for a trip to Wisconsin. It was more like, finish work, cash the checks, throw a bag together and be gone down the road in our Karmann Ghia. There was no stopping for sightseeing or trinket shopping. There were gas stops and junk food. Thirty-three hours later we were there.

The trip didn't seem long. Night turned into day and day turned into night. Next thing you know, we're crossing the Mississippi River into beautiful southwest Wisconsin. I had not been home for three years and the feeling I had crossing that bridge and looking at the Welcome to Wisconsin sign just made me weep. I was so happy. George was happy for me. George was happy for himself too. And so was I. He'd thought I was a prize. I couldn't hardly wait for him to meet my people. That would be the real prize, plus all the bells and whistles. And that's what it was.

Near dawn we reached my sister's place where she lived with her boyfriend. They were still sleeping when we arrived, but jumped out of bed and greeted us with happy faces. Nena was my baby sister. The girl was beautiful from birth. There she stood in her doorway just out of bed half asleep and absolutely stunning. She'd grown from the little teenager I had last seen into this strikingly gorgeous woman. And there alongside her stood the man I'd heard about over and over. They put on a pot of coffee, made us a huge breakfast of venison and eggs and were off to their jobs. George and I crawled in their bed and slept for a few hours. Road weary and a hot meal made for a restful sleep. George was loving Wisconsin and everyone in it. And he'd only met one sister. Next stop, my brothers.

Johnnie lived in an old country schoolhouse on a side road at the outskirts of town. Just riding all the back roads, George felt like he'd died and gone to heaven. June is a great time to travel in Wisconsin. Anytime and all the time is a good time to be in Wisconsin. Johnnie was still at work, but my youngest brother came running out of the house. He'd been recently discharged from the Air Force and was staying there. He looked at me, run right on by and grabbed and hugged George. Although it was their first meeting, it seemed they had always known each other. My brother said, "Hey, nice shirt man." George ripped the snaps open and gave his shirt to my brother. The man that would give his shirt right off his back, that was George.

My sister's wedding was where he met most all my family. It was, to say the least, grandiose. The reception was held on their farm and everyone was there. It seemed like a city, full of people in the front yard. George was beside himself. It was the best time to meet the family—on a special happy occasion. He loved them all and as far as I could tell, they loved him. It was everything I'd hoped for and way more than George ever expected or anticipated. We spent another couple of days enjoying the family and wondering around beautiful Wisconsin before it was time to head back to Arizona and our life there.

We stopped in Chicago to visit all the family there on our way home. More nephews who finished concrete and George's sisters. Getting together with them always meant Palarmos. Pizza and oysters on the half shell. What fun. We weren't able to see everybody, of course, but it was always time well spent. It was time to say our good byes, with tears in our eyes and head west.

Chapter 4

Hobby Farming and Kids

ALL THE WAY BACK, all George could talk about was the next time we'd go back to see the family. He was in love. Not only with me. With my family. With the State of Wisconsin. With himself and the life he'd found. He was dreading going back to fast paced city life, selfish people and traffic. We decided on that trip back to Arizona that there was absolutely no reason we shouldn't become what people called "snowbirds". We put our plan in place. We worked the big jobs, saved as much money as we could and would spend it all in Wisconsin. That's exactly what we did. When we weren't working, we were fishing.

Then came the unexpected. I was involved in a car accident. Someone not paying attention ran a red light and t-boned the Karmann Ghia I was driving. Not only were we without a car, I was not able to work for a while. The insurance company finally settled and another Ghia car was bought. I was for the most part healed and had a fistful of money.

We needed a break, so back to Wisconsin we went, just in time to go fishing. The salmon were spawning on the Sheboygan River. We went for four days. It was not fishing as one might think. It was snagging for salmon. There was no bait or lures. We used heavy sinkers on a long steel swivel leader with a treble hook. Cast out your line and slowly reel back in with jerking motions. Every morning the banks of the river would be lined with people in hip or chest waders. Everyone there for the same reason. At dark, we cleaned fish. At dark thirty the next morning, we were ready to start it all over again. It was fall, and we all know the beauty that Wisconsin offers us at that time of year. It was just fabulous.

Back to Arizona, work, fish and dream about going back to the mid-west.

The following June, we headed back to Wisconsin where we found an old two-story farmhouse and 10 acres for rent. We thought we'd try our hand at hobby farming. First things first though. A coon hound puppy we named Duke. He was 8 weeks old. A brindle plot. Anyone who knows dogs, knows how cute and precious hound puppies are. Duke was no exception.

George had listened to my brothers and all their coon hunting stories and just couldn't hardly wait till Duke was old enough to be part of the pack. He was certain he had the pick of the litter, but my family wasn't so sure as they were strictly blue tick and black and tan owners. And they definitely didn't raise their hounds in the house as lap dogs. But, George was George and that was great by them.

By the full swing of summer, we had a huge array of barnyard animals. We had decided to raise lop-eared rabbits for meat and before that was all said and done, we had over 100 rabbits in the barn in cages. There were 125 laying hens in another barn and 24 turkeys in a covered pen outside. On the other side of the barn we raised 12 feeder pigs and in the pasture we were raising 6 Holstein steers. A pair of geese and a pair of ducks had the run of the whole place. We went to sale barns and bought day old calves and brought them home to bottle feed. Everybody had a name, including the 2 baby lambs. Now all of this sounds great, but the greatest part was the kids.

My brothers and my sister, had already started their own families. We had someone's kids with us nearly all the time. Kids and critters just go together. And it wasn't just my family. George's sisters from Chicago and their kids. At least every other weekend, we'd have family from Chicago and the Wisconsin family together at our place. Everything and everybody was happy and content. Life was great. The animals grew, the garden grew, and our love grew. I was so happy to be there. Happy to be a part of raising the nieces and nephews. I'd never had the chance to be a mom so being near the children was just the best. I was the favorite auntie and George everyone's favorite uncle. It became hard to let the kids go home. They'd cry and we'd cry. We became very attached.

And for whatever reason, there were certain kids that just became part of us. They're the ones that needed something more. They were all special, each of them, but those certain ones just drew us in closer and closer.

John-John was my brother Johnny's son. He was Johnny's oldest child and was the oldest cousin to all my nieces and nephews. I was the oldest of my brothers and sisters and also the oldest cousin on my mother's side of the family. I loved that boy before he was even born. George had great-nephews from Chicago about John-John's age and the things they taught each other over the years was extraordinary. City meets country and what an experience for them and all of us.

Many times all the boys would stay with us for a week or so at a time. They'd have chores to do always before play, so our city boys really got an education about the real world of country living. And although we had plenty of rooms and lots of beds, the boys got introduced to tent life with John-John.

The very first night they decided they'd like to become campers. I was in the kitchen putting bags of food and snacks together for their night out. The boys were upstairs getting their gear ready, when all of the sudden I heard John-John laughing and he shouted out "pajamas—you ain't wearin' no pajamas out there!" I thought I'd die laughing. John-John was a country boy through and through and seemed to have a mission to teach these city boys a thing or two about a thing or two.

Night time in the country consisted of a sky full of stars and a yard light. Earlier in the day Uncle had suggested to them to pitch their tent under the yard light. Although John-John wasn't in favor of the ides, Uncle did know best. Can't imagine how the night would have gone for the other boys who were used to street lights and night lights in every room of their houses in the city!

Uncle stayed awake most of the first night. He could hear them from the front stoop. I guess John-John was the only boy there that had ever peed outside, no tree or nothing, because when one of the other boys announced he was going to the house to use the bathroom, well let's just say that was not going to be tolerated by the little country boy. All night long, they ate, told stories and laughed. The bag of food I'd packed was for sure not your normal camping eats, but it's mostly what I would have wanted to eat if I'd been the one out there. I sent with them a quart jar of homemade dill pickles, a head of crisp cabbage straight from the garden, a full jar of peanut butter, a full bag of chocolate chips and a batch of no bake oatmeal cookies. The bag was empty in the morning.

The city nephews seemed different that next day and not just because they were all tired. Something had changed. It was obvious, because after a long day of helping pull thistles, tall as they were and had supper, they were ready for their bag of snacks and wanting to get back to their tent. It seemed like they'd been together forever and this was just their normal routine.

They'd ride in the bed of the truck with Duke when Uncle had to get feed for the animals and would be singing at the tops of their lungs to Peter, Paul, and Mary, one of Uncle's favorite tapes. They had also learned every word to every Willie song we had.

It was also John-John who taught them about the birds and the bees one day after we'd allowed them to go down and play in the shallow creek in the pasture. The youngest one had always been into bugs and the like, but what he seen that day changed everything. There were frogs everywhere. He came running up to the porch carrying two of them when he called out to Uncle in total amazement—"look Uncle, they are on top of one another." It was the little country boy that informed him later in the tent that night, the why, how come, and what for about that!

Each time the boys would come to the country, they'd have to eventually go home. It was tough, on the kids and on us. If they'd have had their rathers, they'd have just lived there forever. It was always a huge long weekend party whenever their parents came for them. The parents, of course, were George's nieces and nephews, many of them my age, who had loved Uncle all their lives and were so happy to be able to have their own kids enjoy and know Uncle. Their knowing and loving him was a very different experience than the one their children were having.

When they were youngsters, Uncle had been a very different man. It was in those days that George had been drunk most of the time. They seen him at his best and worst. His best, being not totally wasted, still a happy and playful Uncle with a whiskey breathe. He'd let them get away with things that their parents wouldn't. He had a different way of talking and helping the kids through difficult times than their parents. Unfortunately, they also seen him in drunken rages. Truth is, kids are resilient. As unbecoming or unfitting as that may have been, many of them learned valuable life lessons despite his cantankerous ways.

We enjoyed the last days of fall. We harvested the garden, did the butchering, sold the other farm animals, and closed up the farmhouse to head back to warm, sunny Arizona before winter had a chance to rear its ugly head. It wasn't only time to leave before the snow started to fly, but also time to start making money so we could do it all over again come the following spring. Duke got to stay in Wisconsin for the winter. The city would be no place for a coon hound. George was lonely for him before we even got to the Iowa border. Me too.

We were looking forward to getting back to work, seeing our Arizona and Colorado families and our friends. We were also excited to get back to our fishing car. We had decided on the trip back that we would need some rest before starting back to work, so we'd need to go fishing for a few days first. We had missed the beautiful lakes while we were farming.

Soon as we were back in Phoenix, we had the car serviced and headed to Lake Pleasant. Our first stop before getting there was the Italian store. Nearly every fishing trip, we took the same lunch. We'd stop and get the black wrinkled olives for George, the green olives with onions and carrots for me and of course, imported provolone and a crusty bread loaf. It was the perfect food for fishing. A bite of cheese, a bite of bread, and an olive. Lunch really doesn't get any better than that. Also if it happened to be a Tuesday or Thursday, we'd stop at a Dunkin Donuts and buy a sweet treat for the girl at the entrance gate. We'd trade with her. Donuts and Pepsi for a day's free pass into the lake.

We did as we had planned. Fished for a week and then started back to work. We both stayed busy. We were not necessarily on the same jobs all the time. Everything was back to normal. We were paying rent in Arizona and still paying rent to keep our farmhouse in Wisconsin. We were excited that the landlord was putting in a new furnace. Our blood was thin living in the desert southwest. We had the furnace on even in June. I had asked someone to go to the farmhouse to check on everything for us. Just to make sure. Well the call came back and everything wasn't so good. Evidently the landlord was taking his good ole sweet time to install the furnace, so he had shut off the power to the whole house. And three weeks later, when he finished, he turned the power back on. In a matter of three weeks, every single package of meat in our freezer had spoiled. There was a side of pork, a side of beef, rabbits, chickens, turkeys, berries, and vegetables. Blood and berry juice thawed and refroze. We would have to deal with it when we returned, and that hopefully the landlord would keep his hands off the power switch.

Chapter 5

Memorial Day 1987

GEORGE AND I AND Michael and Susie not only fished for fun, we also played cards. It was either Canasta or Cribbage. We would play all night long. One evening after card playing all night, we stopped by George's sister's house. She met us in her driveway. She appeared shaken and nervous. She said she had just received a phone call from Wisconsin. The news she said was not good. My brother, Johnnie, was hanging a tire swing for his 2 year old daughter. A branch broke. He fell 19 feet to his death. I believe I went into shock. This couldn't even be happening. I remember George trying to console me, but I was dazed. I wasn't even believing that this was really happening.

George's sister went into the kitchen and came back out handing him $87.00 from her cookie jar. We got in our car and headed straight to Wisconsin. It was Memorial Day weekend. The drive seemed to take forever. And still I was making no sense of this. We arrived at my sister's house just as they were getting ready to go to Johnnie's wake.

We left for the funeral home and met my brother Scottie. It wasn't until actually seeing Johnnie in a coffin that I realized how true this really was happening. And, OH MY GOD, my brother is gone. OH MY GOD. This is not in proper order. I am the oldest, I should be the one to go first. OH MY GOD. But eventually life goes on and everyone must adjust in order to maintain a healthy course. And so it goes.

George and I had decided to sell out from our farmhouse. We did it by way of auction. It was a really fun time. The auctioneer sang great and people were buying. They bought everything, except our memories.

Back in Phoenix, we continued on with fishing and finishing concrete. Arizona is the place to be for year round entertainment for us. Fishing or finishing concrete.

It was during this time when union finishers were allowed to use walking tools. It sure made life easier. No more knee boards. Stand near the edge, stretched out 3 handles long, wiping out the floors right behind George, the machine man. We became quite the team and could handle a lot of concrete between the two of us. And we made it fun. Oh, he would still point like he always did and say things like, "damn girl, who taught you to do work like that", knowing of course that would be him. Life was good on the slab.

October proved to be a very exciting month for us. Out of the blue, George asked me to marry him. Without hesitation, I accepted. Near the end of the month, we went to Las Vegas. Michael was the best man and George's sister, K.A., was my matron of honor. It was a beautiful short ceremony in a quaint little wedding chapel. George and I were married. Life was good in the romance department.

Life was good on the lake too. Christmas Eve day, I caught a 6 pound bass at Lake Pleasant. OH MY GOD, George was so proud. He handed over all 3 quarters without even spitting on them first.

We got in the fishing car and headed straight to the bowling alley where George's sister and brother-in-law were bowling. I was so proud to show them and their bowling team and the others in the bowling alley. It was a fun time. I believe we stopped at 3 more friends homes to show off that bass before we finally got home to clean it and throw it in the hot pan.

Chapter 6

The Little Red Schoolhouse

ONE EVENING AT HOME, my sister calls to inform us about a place that would be coming up for rent soon. Then she told us the place. Well don't you know, it was an old one room schoolhouse turned into a 2 bedroom home, surrounded by mature trees, and fields and pastures on all sides of a one acre plot. Also right in direct line of great coyote hunting. We'll come back to the coyote hunting later. We of course said, "oh hell yes!". So arrangements were put together and in April, George and I moved to Wisconsin into the little red schoolhouse.

I tended to the house and property while George worked either out of the Chicago or Dixon locals.

Monthly we would visit family in Chicago and yearly we would visit family in Colorado. And all the time we would be visiting the family in Wisconsin.

Although George had it all going on for himself, there was still a dark side to him. Every now and then something strange would come over him and consume him for days. Then just like turning on a light switch, he would come back like nothing ever happened. I got used to it finally after I figured out I was not the cause. I was what made him come back. I never questioned. I never felt like it was my place to ask. A person just knows.

George made friends easily and soon became a full fledged coyote hunter. Duke never made the cut, but George did because he brought the sandwiches.

Now this is a winter time sport. They drive around in trucks with dogs and tracking collars and walkie talkies and thermos full of hot coffee and a pint of brandy in the glove box.

They follow a farmer spreading manure early in the morning and wait for the coyotes to show up to forage through the spread. First come the Bald Eagles. They get their fill and then the coyotes.

The hunters let their dogs loose and the chase is on. Everybody's getting their exercise for the day. They may run one or they may run half a dozen coyotes a day. Keeps everybody entertained through the fridges of the Wisconsin winters.

I forgot to mention, they also do this driving around with the windows wide open so they can listen for the hounds. George is freezing. Never has he known such cold-ever. But, he loved it. He learned how to dress for the cold.

Over the years that passed, George and Father Winter made friends. George loved being outside doing something or doing nothing at all.

There was a camaraderie among the hunters who were all friends and had known one another as youngsters. Some were cousins. Always a meeting at the local bar to discuss the day's hunt and plan for the next hunt.

There really were other things he enjoyed and that was our kids. Well, they were other people's children, but they were our kids. We were extremely fortunate to be able to be around when the babies were born. Nieces and nephews and neighborhood children too. We bonded with the children. Mostly all of the time, but I'd be lying if I said all. You know, every family has one or two.

George had a way about him that kids loved. He didn't ever talk kid talk. He talked the way he talked and they all understood. He taught them things they would never have otherwise learned. He loved sardines (either in mustard or tomato sauce) laid out perfectly end to end on a celery stalk. The kids loved it too. I couldn't even stand to be in the house when they were eating that! He ate ice cream with a fork straight out of the bucket. He liked Jolly Rancher hard candy. The kids loved it all too.

When he went squirrel hunting, he'd take a thermos of hot coffee and potato and egg sandwiches. And whoever was lucky enough to go hunting with Uncle would get to drink coffee.

We made a game out of raking leaves in the fall. We burned them as we raked and everyone got schooled on proper fire rules. They all got to use the poker as Uncle stood herd giving directions for proper poking of a backyard fire. George would get his accordion and play old Italian music for me and kid songs that all the youngsters sang along to. Duke laying close to George all the time.

Decorating for Christmas was the best. One Christmas tree inside, one Christmas tree outside. The one inside, I decorated with ribbons and bows and flowers grown in my garden that had been dried, and the lights. Beautiful enough, but what was under the tree was even more beautiful. I created a Christmas village. There were houses and a bakery and a fire station, the post office and hardware store. Many of these buildings lit up. A complete farm set with all the animals, fences, the barn and the silos. There was also the train. Smoke came billowing out as it chugged along an 8 foot track. The best. The kids all loved playing under the tree. What fun!

New Year's Eve was always our biggest and best time of the holidays. At 4:00 in the afternoon on New Year's Eve, we had the parents of all the kids, usually between 11 and 13 all total, drop the kids off by us. That allowed them to go out for their own special New Year's Eve parties. It worked out well for everyone.

I cooked a full big holiday dinner; turkey, dressing, mashed potatoes, gravy, cranberries—all things. Pumpkin pie for dessert.

After the kids got everything washed and put away, they took the table and chairs out of the kitchen. Uncle turned the lights down a little and turned on country music. Well, the little girls were all out there jumping around, acting like little girls act.

George asked me to dance—you know, the old fashioned, take a lady by her hand to the dance floor, bow to her and begin dancing away. George and I were as wonderful dancing together as we were with everything else in our life. So the kids stood in amazement as we covered the kitchen dance floor several times.

That was the night the boys were schooled on the proper way to ask a girl for a dance. The girls were introduced to the way of excepting the invitation for a dance. We tried teaching the box step and that night they all got it. If any of them ever remembered after that night is anybody's guess.

Throughout the evening we had snacks to eat and pop or hot cocoa to drink. Usually about an hours worth of dancing and we would have all had enough of that.

Time now for the kids Christmas program for us. Between the different families there, they were from 3 different schools. Each little school had a grade school Christmas program with little skits and old fashioned Christmas carols. So these kids would each take their turns, school by school and sing us songs. A few songs they all sang together. It was just so wonderful. We were all so blessed.

We would all watch the ball drop down in New York City and toast with Champagne glasses filled with sparkling non-alcoholic champagne. Happy New Year. Hugs and kisses—put your glasses in the sink very carefully and we would call it a night. What Fun!

Next morning, New Year's Day, after a huge full breakfast, the parents would come by and pick up their kids.

During the winter months, George enjoyed coyote hunting, squirrel and cottontail hunting. He didn't care much about the whole ice fishing thing. But as soon as we could get on the river, it was catfishing as usual. He had a partner named Bear too, that he'd go with when I had other things to do. And fished they did. Once they'd get home at dark thirty then they'd have to skin and clean the fish, then bag and freeze them. Next day, they'd do it all once again.

One afternoon while they were out fishing and I was in the garden I heard screeching tires. I ran to the road and there on the road next to the milk truck, laid Duke. OH MY GOD. He wasn't dead, but his breathing was labored. I loaded him in our truck and drove to the feed mill in town a few miles away.

There were always guys in there, some hunters, who might be able to tell me what to do. One of the hunters helped Duke stand and examined his legs, his head, and chest. There was no blood, but was sure that the ribs were broken and probably punctured his lungs. Two hours later, Duke died.

I sat on the tail gate with Duke in the bed of the truck covered with a blanket, waiting for George and Bear. I didn't know how I'd tell George. All I could do was cry. Before long, I could hear them coming down the road. As soon as George got out of the truck, he looked around for Duke, who was normally waiting for him to get home. He called him. No Duke. Then he looked at me and walked to our truck.

He uncovered Duke and just started weeping. I grabbed two shovels and Bear and I walked to the back corner of the property and began to dig a grave for Duke. Neither of us spoke. When we were done, I looked up and here was George carrying Duke in his arms. He laid him in that grave, got a shovel and filled it in. OH MY GOD.

When they started cleaning the fish, I told them what had happened. The truck driver was just sick over it, although it certainly wasn't his fault. No matter what we did, we could not keep Duke from chasing trucks. So one day, a truck just got him. That's all.

George was lost without Duke. He kept asking all the hunters if any of them knew about plot puppies for sale. Well, as luck would have it, one of them did know about a litter about 8 weeks old. Oh great. I really did not want another dog. Sure enough, George called the guy and he would be expecting us in the morning. He would give George the pick of the litter because he was a friend of a friend.

Early the following morning, we were up at the crack of dawn and on the road. Four hours later we arrived. There were hound dogs barking all over the place. The guy took us into the area where the puppies were all rolling around, jumping all over each other and basically just acting like puppies.

George stepped over the make shift pen and no sooner did when one of the puppies went straight to him without any prompting. It happened to be a little male. That's the one. George did not pick. The puppy picked George.

I still wasn't keen on the whole idea. I missed Duke. Well I was the one to hold the new puppy all the way home, and at some point, I made the statement, he'll never be any more than just a shadow of Duke. Well with that, we named him Shadow. He became our new lap dog. He was house-broken in about three weeks.

That's when a call from someone else came to see if George wanted a little female plot puppy also 8 weeks old. We went and brought her home. We named her Sheba.

Two coon hound puppies in the house. Shadow seemed a little jealous at the beginning and I remember thinking, I sure hope he doesn't have a mean streak in him.

George wanted them both to be good hounds that he could take hunting. He would catch a raccoon in a live trap and hook it up to the riding lawn mower. He'd mow the grass while the pups were running behind barking and chasing after the raccoon in the cage. This went on for months.

Comes time to start coon hunting, and the men pick up George and Shadow. Shadow didn't make the cut. He didn't seem to get along well with the other dogs. Next time it was Sheba's turn to go out. She didn't do much other than stay right next to George. Even though they didn't make the grade, we loved them anyways.

After coon season was over, then was deer hunting. Another sport George loved. The biggest event of all the hunting seasons. It started the weekend before Thanksgiving and ended the weekend after. It was daily hunting from daylight till dark. At night there was skinning, butchering, grinding, and wrapping. It was a lot of work, but the pay off of meat in the freezer made it all worthwhile.

We also kept some carcasses to throw out in an empty field not more than the length of a football field from our picture window

I Listened For His Breath

in the living room. Every day we could sit on the couch and watch as everyone took their turns chewing on what was left. First would come the Bald Eagles, second, the coyotes, and after that the crows. What fun.

Chapter 7

The Diagnoses

GEORGE NEEDED TO HAVE a hernia repaired that had been giving him issues all winter. Arrangements were made, surgery was done, and he was home laying on the couch when his surgeon called. He wanted us to come back to his office because he needed to show us something. We went, reluctantly, because George felt so bad.

The doctor showed us the x-rays of George's lungs. One side had a spot the size of a dime, the other side a spot the size of a quarter. The surgeon had already consulted with the other doctors and had been in contact with the University hospital about 90 miles away. He told us that George had lung cancer. He went on to explain the urgency of starting treatment. The x-rays had already been sent to Madison to the oncology department and they concluded George should start immediately.

They had gone so far as to schedule George for his first chemotherapy and radiation treatments to begin the following week. After about a half hour of listening, George stood up, reached across the desk to shake the doctor's hand and said—"thank you for telling me what I've got and no to all of your treatments." With that, he turned and walked out of the office. I got up to follow him and the doctor was telling me I had to change my husband's mind, that I had to get him to Madison. Finally, I said to him, "didn't you hear what he just said? No and no is what he means. He will live until he doesn't anymore. As far as he is concerned, he will live a lot longer without any of these treatments. It's his decision. I hope that if need be, you will prescribe pain medications for him as he needs them." To which the doctor replied that he would have NOTHING to do with this. If George would not go through treatments as prescribed that he should find another doctor.

A couple of days later, George got a fever and the site of the hernia surgery was red and hot to the touch. To the emergency room we go where they drew out a large amount of really stinky pus. It would take months to heal over.

We were being seen by our local doctor, who insisted on some blood tests specific to the diagnosis of lung cancer. All those tests were positive. A lot to deal with for the two of us, not to mention our families and friends.

I asked no questions of George because I knew he had always felt that it was not cancer that killed, it was the treatments given. However George wanted to handle this news was up to him. We had to tell people. We had to tell the kids.

George and I started a cancer and death and dying education, not only for the two of us, but for everyone we loved. George spoke openly about cancer. He said the word Cancer out loud and made everyone feel at ease to talk about it to him. That included the kids. They worried about Uncle because they loved him so much. He was kind, funny, firm and could be a wonderful teacher when needed. They wanted to be informed. Spending time with him, they would see for themselves and become informed.

Time was drawing near for George's birthday. I had an idea about a surprise party for him. KIDS ONLY! The kids were all excited and were promised to secrecy. The big day finally came. None of the kids had said a word to Uncle. I told him I needed to run up town and pick up a few things, that I wouldn't be long. I called him from the neighbor's house and told him to look out the kitchen window. There were eleven kids climbing barbed wire fences then began running, holding hands, laughing and calling out Happy Birthday to Uncle. That pasture, all tall and green, was about 2 football fields long and ended at our back yard where they crossed another barbed wire fence.

They were happy, laughing, thirsty and tired. They all had made something for Uncle's presents. That was all in my car and the cake in the trunk. I had a store bought cake, decorated of course, but the kids had also baked and decorated a cake. Some of the bigger kids unloaded the car and all the rest of us went in the house. The kids were so excited to have Uncle open up the presents. So he sat in his favorite chair, the kids either on the floor by him or on the couch next to him.

Each family of kids taking turns to present their gift. It was so beautiful to watch, hoping silently that we get to continue these fun filled times for a long, long time, also knowing, time could be very short.

He would be so gracious with tears welling. Then they would hug him and say they loved him. One of his gifts he really loved was a purple tee shirt with the three little girls' hand prints painted in white. He wore the shirt a lot. Presents are over and now it's time to eat.

I made George's favorite meal. Spaghetti and meatballs and neck bones. That also happened to be each of the kids' favorite too. Pasta for thirteen. He shared the neck bones, because he had taught each one of them how to eat them. Pork neck bones that the meat falls right off the bone. Everybody is about finished with pasta and now it's time for the cakes. Out comes the store bought cake with his name on it and yes he liked it. Then comes one of the bigger kids carrying the cake the kids made. The cake was chocolate layered and frosted with a chocolate frosting. Each kid got to put what they thought Uncle would like on his birthday cake. OH MY GOD. The cake was adorned with gummy worms and gummy bears, M&Ms, tiny pretzels, a can of sardines sat on the top, raisins, and cereal that spelled out Happy Birthday Uncle and a fishing lure. Guess which cake got cut first. George kept going back to the presents. Some kids had made their mothers take them to the store so they could buy Uncle something with their own money. So besides the wonderful homemade gifts were fishing lures that he was partial to and three tubs of stink bait. He just couldn't believe all the things he got from the kids. He was overwhelmed.

After the parents had picked up their kids that afternoon, they returned later that evening for the grown- ups party. George had a great BIRTHDAY PARTY. It was in everyone's mind if we'd get to enjoy more birthdays with him or not. No one ever questioned his decision not to do any treatments. Even if they had disagreed, they never once said anything to him or to me.

None of us knew what to expect, including George. We just continued to live our lives the way we always had been doing.

George and I had a lot to consider. He needed to go back to Phoenix for one thing. There was business he needed to take care of with the union hall. He wanted to retire and start collecting his pension that he had worked 38 years for. So we flew him to Phoenix, where Michael picked him up and took George to his house. They would go together to the hall and same as before, either take a job or go fishing.

George was at Michael's mercy, without a vehicle of his own. Every day he would call me. He started feeling sick and not himself while he was out there, but still had work to do to get his pension.

It seemed that the by-laws were such that pensions were not paid out until the finisher had started to collect their social security. I always figured the pension was not paid before social security because they'd hoped the finisher would be dead before they were of age to collect. And that had mostly been the case. So basically what that meant for George, was that after 38 years of working, he would be screwed in the end. He was not of the age yet to be retired by social security standards. And yet, he was living with a terminal disease, that would surely take his life before he turned 65.

He ended up staying there for three months. After endless meetings, George finally got the by-laws rewritten. This was going to help everyone in the union in the end. It allowed George to be able to draw his pension before the social security disability started to pay.

He could now return home and not have to stress about how we would live without him working. He was sick and weary when he did get home. He had lost weight and was so tired. He was happy to be home among family and friends. Once we got settled back into one another and everything around us kind of settled down, it was time to hear all about his trip to Arizona. Since he had been home for only a few days, I now noticed things. Things that were different with George.

He would moan in his sleep as if in pain. It seemed a long time between his breaths. In the mornings, he was not his normal chipper self. He would want breakfast, but then a half hour or so later, I could hear him throwing up in the bathroom. And then come out and act like nothing ever happened. I mentioned to him finally, that the doctor's office had called while he was away and wondered how he was doing and that when he got back to make an appointment to see him. George said yes. I right away made the appointment for the following morning. That was all good with George.

The ole doc looked surprised when he seen George. The doc asked questions and George truthfully answered. It was all just breaking my heart. We left with some prescriptions of some very serious drugs. With no insurance or social security benefits yet (even in a terminal condition) we were watching George's pension start to dwindle.

I had no clue about the severity of his pain. We had stomach pills and pain patches of morphine. He just laid low for about a week after starting the medicines until he was able to handle things again. The stomach pills allowed him to eat without heart burn or sour stomach. He would still be nauseated and pucky at times for no particular reason. The patch took away the pain and that allowed him to be able to do things outside again. He was happy again in the mornings and rearing to go. He loved going to my brother's place and splitting wood. Gas splitter, stumps, peacefulness, and George. He did it for months and months. A few days at a time.

He'd work till he couldn't anymore, then he'd stay home, get nursed back to health and go again. His cough was getting worse now and his breathing heavier. He would still be in the bathroom vomiting. The poor man, I couldn't do anything.

During all this same time, my sister Nena had discovered a lump on her breast. She had called me when she first found it and thought she had bumped it when she fell down a day earlier. She had been carrying a wooden box with garden tools and such in it, when she fell and landed right on top of it. Still she didn't know about that either. It felt like a hard pea inside her. I told her maybe she should have it looked at. She called me again and asked if I'd go with her to the appointment she had made for the following day with a surgeon in Dubuque, Iowa. My first impression of her doctor was not that great. I thought he was an arrogant asshole. Nena loved him. He gave her two options after examining her. His thought was to just keep an eye on it and have it reexamined in three months, that it was probably nothing at all to worry about. The second option was to have the lump biopsied. Nena went with the first idea. She thanked him over and over again. There was not one single thing I liked about him, his office, his staff or his waiting room. I could not find a good feeling anywhere and yet sister was so happy that he did not seem concerned at all. The feel good for Nena did not last long. About a week later, she made another appointment to have a biopsy done, just to be on the safe side. No bruise ever showed up, making her doubt that the lump had anything to do with her fall. The procedure was done and her doctor had the findings. Breast Cancer. Aggressive in young women. Nena was 35 years old. OH MY GOD! Sister was hysterical. I wanted to reach across that doctor's desk and just choke him. Well, we wouldn't have him any more as a doctor, now we'd get an oncologist. She was seen right away by the new doctor and was being given information so quickly there was no time to absorb anything. She was so scared. She just wanted to do whatever he said to get this cancer out of her body. This doctor did have a different way about his approach to his layout for treatment. He kept saying aggressive over and over.

I Listened For His Breath

Every time he did, my sister just cringed. She didn't have time to think about anything. They wanted to begin radiation treatment immediately. She agreed.

There were to be 21 treatments. Who knew anything about breast cancer questions to ask or radiation? What is it? What does it do? Where does it go? What happens during treatment? What happens after treatment? How soon do you know if treatment worked? If the cancer is gone after treatment, will it stay gone? If the cancer did not respond to treatment, well, then what? All great questions that neither Nena or her husband or me even had time to think of, let alone ask. It all just happened so fast.

Conversation on the way back home that day was like walking on broken glass. We just let Nena go on and on. She was mad, she was scared and just so pissed off. She was also glad she had that doctor. She liked him.

We all got back to my house where George patiently waited to hear the news. We left George and Nena alone at the kitchen table talking. For Nena, it was like having to get George's approval of what she had decided to do. She was a very respectful girl and loved George tremendously. She knew good and well what George had decided to do, nothing. She knew he had an attitude, for himself, about treatments. Nena didn't need his approval, but she asked him for it anyway. She cried. He cried. He ended up telling her that he would drive her to treatment everyday. I guess they both laughed at that, because George was way too sick for that. She had his best well wishes though. The two of them had become thick as thieves since she was diagnosed. Together they had cancer in common. I was always so glad that they had each other. George's attitude was inspiring to her and to all of us. He was non-judgmental. He kept his personal opinion to himself and shared it only with me. His positive attitude was very uplifting to sister and she drew off his energy.

After they left for their house, George and I discussed everything I'd heard and witnessed during the day. He hated that my sister was having to deal with cancer. We talked about how all this was going to happen. It was a hundred miles one way trip five days a week for three weeks of radiation to her left breast. We decided that I could and should go with her. Her husband worked, their oldest son was in school and either George or Grandma would watch the youngest until we'd get back each day. Nena was home every day when the school bus got there. She made everything work at her house and I made everything work at mine. George's doctor increased the strength of the morphine patch and added a morphine pill for SUDDEN onset pain. That helped.

After the scheduled radiation was over, Nena's breast was purple and as hard as a rock. The doctor was certain that she would need no more treatments and she was good to go. He'd see her back in six months. Great.

Now we could get our households back to normal routines again. At least as normal as two houses can be with serious health issues.

I could see that George was feeling a little better each day. I wondered if it was just because I was home again all day. I didn't care what the reason, I was happy about it and so was he. He felt so good that we decided to take a trip to Colorado to visit the family.

We drove the eighteen hour trip straight through like we always did. George slept most of the way. The elevation of the Rockies was harmful to his breathing, but he just kept up his pace never letting anyone see him sweat. Once we got there, George would again go with the nephews. To just be on the job with the boys, meant everything to him. The nieces and I would bring lunch to the job. Sometimes I'd even get to pick up the walking trowel and help them out while they ate. At night, the family bowled. They were all on leagues, so we'd hang out in the bowling alley watching the big kids bowl and the little kids running all over. And what bowlers they were. Didn't matter. Men or women. They were all great. The pins didn't stand a chance.

Colorado is where George got introduced to oxygen. One of the nephews was on oxygen and so was his dad (George's brother). They both had their oxygen on and trying to tell George how much it helped and that he should try it. Well, eventually he did and so there sat all three men on oxygen. And all three smoking. What a sight! I was thrilled that they eased him into it. Maybe that would mean he'd allow it at home. He slept with oxygen on that night and slept all night long without struggling for breath.

We threw George a surprise birthday party while we were there. A sister from Chicago and a sister from Phoenix also came. Hugs and kisses were all around. Italians are very special people.

It was all stressful. Even though it was all good stress, it still took a toll on George. It was time to head back to Wisconsin and see Shadow and Sheba.

George slept most of the way home. My thoughts were all over. I had so many questions and no answers. George and Nena. Nena and George. With winter approaching I wondered if we'd get through the upcoming holidays without incident.

George's doctor added another morphine patch. He had lost several more pounds and still the violent heaving. It was black and smelled bad. We figured the cancer had spread.

In January, we had a phone call that George's mother had passed away. Her body was to be flown from Phoenix to Chicago, where she would be buried next to her husband. As is old tradition, she was waked two nights and funeral and burial on the third day. Everyone went to all three. There was a Catholic mass for her and graveside service. Beautiful. All of this was very hard on George. Seeing everybody. Talking to everybody for three days was a lot on him. George never got over losing his mother. He truly loved her.

It was a long winter. George sick all the time. But when someone would come over to visit, he'd hold it all together. The family loved to play dice. The games were mostly at our house because of the long beautiful table George had built. There were times though that if he wasn't right, he'd just excuse himself and go lay on the couch. He was still in the same room. The family was there a couple of times when George had to throw up. Violent is the only word to describe it. We all felt totally helpless. There was nothing at all that we could do. The best thing, was all just be together.

The summer fishing hours got shorter and shorter. George just couldn't handle being in the boat for long. However long he wanted to be out, that's how it was, no matter who was with him. We were all taking care of George.

Late fall a horrific accident happened to our little farming community. I was washing dishes when I started seeing flashing red lights. We looked out the front window and vehicle after vehicle with their lights flashing and sirens screaming. They were all going right next door to us. OH MY GOD! After the last of them, we followed behind. We parked up by the house. All the attention was on one large drying bin. We asked. The auger wasn't working right. Charlie climbed to the top and crawled in with wrenches to fix it. For whatever reason, Charlie got buried under twenty tons of corn. People were digging corn with their hands. Men were cutting holes in the sides of the steel silo. The bobcats were scooping corn and moving it to make room for more. Family, friends, and neighbors digging with whatever they had. And then the digging stopped. A young man, in his early thirties, husband and father of three young boys, gone. The boys had been in the house with me. Their mom did not want then outside during the search. When she came back to the house, it was to tell her boys that their daddy had passed away and gone to heaven. OH MY GOD!

The entire community turned out for the services of this young farmer, who loved his wife and loved his kids. One of three brothers, all farmers. Such a tragic accident and a warning about how quickly farming accidents can happen.

After George's mother passed, he really started going downhill. His oldest sister was also having some very serious health issues. George and I stayed in touch with her by phone at least weekly. They comforted each other for sure; the oldest sister and the baby brother.

The following winter, in February, a phone call came. It was Chicago. George's sister had passed away. OH MY GOD! While he was on the phone, he was also looking out the picture window watching Shadow being very mean to Sheba. Shadow had showed signs of this before.

George got off the phone. He hugged and kissed me and told me to start packing. He said he was going to go outside and see what the problem was with the dogs. I mentioned that Shadow had come after me the week before, for absolutely no reason. So George goes out and was walking towards the dogs when Shadow went after him and actually grabbed him on the forearm and didn't want to let go. All the while, he was mean growling. George shook him loose finally and walked backwards to the house. He went into the bedroom and came out with the .45. He went back out towards the garage to get a shovel. He went near where Duke was buried, and began digging another grave. I called Sheba inside and Shadow was just in the yard. After George got done digging, he called Shadow to him. He came, but he was growling and showing his teeth to George. When he lunged toward George, he took a bullet and fell right in the hole. Sheba would be sad, hell, we'd all be sad, but we couldn't have a mean dog around us or the kids. I had a feeling when we first got Shadow that he might have a mean streak. He was four years old.

Again to Chicago for a funeral. OH MY GOD! We stayed only a couple of days. Excitement and stress caused severe shortness of breath. Scary. Very scary. A lot of it had to do with the city and traffic. Over the years he had grown to really dislike Chicago. It was a rare event that we would even go there after he got sick.

When we did get home, George could hardly wait to see Sheba. Our pet sitter said while we were away, she never ate or drank and just seemed lifeless. He was right. She was a very depressed little girl. She missed Shadow, even he was so mean to her in the end. She eventually came back around and was with George wherever he was.

Chapter 8

Fulfilling Sacraments

ON ONE OF THOSE snowy mornings while we were having our coffee, George announced to me that he'd like for us to be married in the Catholic Church. I wasn't too surprised at that. I, of course, said okay and I'll put those plans in place. It meant an annulment for me. I didn't know what that would entail, but it would have to get done.

George, being very old fashioned, needed to fulfill his sacraments, through the church. Those would be a marriage and to be anointed before death. It is what he believed in, no matter what.

I drove to town and went right to the rectory of St. Thomas Catholic Church. Father Bud greeted me. We knew each other, although not well. I knew him basically through others. I asked for a moment of his time and so we went into his office. I explained what was happening at my house. He had no idea. I explained further that I would like him to stop in from time to time and visit with George. I needed to secure a couple of documents and when I had them, I was to return to see him. It was all going to be good.

While I waited for documents, I started planning a wedding. OH MY GOD. One of George's twin sisters had been my matron of honor in Las Vegas, so I asked the other twin in Chicago to be the matron for this ceremony. She happily agreed.

The papers came and the annulment was granted. A date was then made. It was an evening wedding in our gorgeous Catholic church. Afterwards we went back to our house and everyone enjoyed the hot Italian beef sandwiches and cake I had made.

A few months later, we all found out that the twin sister from Chicago had lung cancer. It happens that I was very close to my sister-in-law. Every chance I got in between George and Nena, I would head to Chicago to be with her and care for her over a weekend, and sometimes for a week at a time.

Of course, during these couple of years, George was getting thinner and thinner, sleeping a lot and waking up unable to catch a breath. We'd jump in the truck in the middle of the night and roll the windows down so the air would blow right in his face. I'd bring up oxygen again and he would bark. So I waited.

Nena had gone through many sessions of radiation and chemotherapy after a total mastectomy. She continued the fight and I was with her every day.

On the weekends, I would usually go to Chicago. My sister-in-law continued to loose ground. She had done one treatment of chemo and decided no more of that. She did have some drugs for nausea and depression, a tranquilizer and a sleeping pill. When I was there, the medicines also included hot teas, biscotti, massages and me, a great listener. A call came late one night from her son pleading for me to come, his mother was asking for me. I made sure everything was okay with my own sister and with George. He worried about me driving the four hours to Chicago in the middle of the night, but was happy and proud that I would go to tend to his sister. Nena would be alright too. She had her husband and our other sister.

I packed my little bag and headed down the road. I cried for the first twenty miles because I already missed George. Nobody could take care of him like I did.

I walked into my sister-in-law's house and smelled death. I went to her and watched her as she slept. She had retained a lot of water since I saw her last week and I could also hear faintly the gurgling as her breaths were very shallow. This was not good. Her son left to get to the police academy as he was a student there. I asked him to stay, but he did not want to. I told him that his mother's time to pass had come. I explained that because of the things I had noticed since I got there, that I didn't believe she would make it through the night. When he said no, I understood that to mean that he would rather not be present. Of which I totally understood. Some of us can do this and some cannot. Care giving is a tough job, and not everyone can handle all the aspects of it. This, of course, includes death and dying.

Off he went to the police academy where he was near to graduating. We were all so proud. His mother beamed with pride. She also had the fear, of course, that a mother would have. Always praying for God to watch over and protect him.

When she woke up, she was happy to see me sitting there. She told me things she needed to get done that her son would have to take care of. We made some small talk and she was ready for another nap. I didn't usually sleep when I was watching over someone, but I did then. I thought it was a light sleep, but I don't know. It seemed like I kept waking up to look at her. Everything seemed fine. One time, though, it was very different. I had opened my eyes and instantly was drawn to her ring. It was just sparkling. Then the room turned a beautiful translucent blue. I could see her dancing with a man, but she was still laying on the bed. I laid there on that little loveseat and did not even move. I don't know if I was even breathing. And then just like that, the room was back to normal. Now I really was awake. I listened for her breath. It was slower and slower. When she woke, I asked her if she had been dreaming. She smiled lovingly and said, "Oh, yes. I was dancing with my husband." I asked her about her pretty ring she was wearing and she told me he had given it to her many years ago. I told her what I had gotten to see. She felt like it was a sign and that he was waiting for her and fell back to sleep. I went to the kitchen to light the white candle. I put the Italian music on very low and sat with her and prayed. She moaned and groaned in pain and could not get comfortable. Her handsome son, in his police uniform, got home and headed to his room to change clothes. I was sitting on the bed holding her hand when she drew that last breath. I believe she waited for him to come home before she passed.

I went to tell her son and explained to him the urgency to take care of a few things. He quickly left. After he was gone, I called 911. I said what I said, but it didn't make any difference. It seemed like every fire truck, ambulance, and cop car were all in front of her house and I had to explain. I didn't want all the noise and hoopla, but that's the way they do it in Chicago. While the professionals were in the house, I took time to call George. He was bad off and worse when I told him about his sister. I told him that as soon as I could, I'd drive home and bring him back. We would stay at his sister's house.

After the body was removed, all the calls were made and the house was put back together, I left to get home to George. I could hardly wait to cross the state line and be back in the farmland. I started cooking as soon as I got home. I made sauce and meatballs. I made a pot of chili. George loved being in the house when it smelled like an Italian deli.

We packed the car. The Nesco roasters of sauce and chili got loaded in the trunk. George did not feel good. He did not want to drive. I jumped in the driver's seat and away we went. Four hours later, we where there. The house was full of family. I kept thinking on the drive all the way down that the stress George would be under wasn't going to be good. He wasn't right as it was even in the beautifulness of his own home. I also figured he'd want to act as if everything was great with him. I would have to be the one to tell everyone, everything else. He hung in there pretty damn good considering. His other sister flew in from Arizona. This would be very rough on her, burying her twin sister. They had lost their oldest sister only two months prior. Now they are here for their baby sister. OH MY GOD! The service was sad but beautiful. When we got back to the house, George was not good. It was hard for him to breathe. This made him nervous and hyper and then really hard to catch a breath. After we finally helped him just settle down and breathe, we loaded back up and headed home. George slept most of the way, but he sure enough woke up when we were crossing the state line and were back in Wisconsin. Then right back to sleep.

Being home, made George feel better. Sheba was so happy that we were back too. She laid right next to George.

I made an appointment to see the doctor. He decided to give George morphine pills and morphine liquid. Once he got going on it, he got results. The pain was not as bad but he slept all the time. But you trade one thing for the other.

My sister, Nena, was in really tough shape. George and I drove over to her house, about thirty miles, shortly after we got home from Chicago. Nena felt so bad for George about losing another sister. Nena knew her too, and was very saddened by her passing. George and Nena visited together in the living room. I busied myself doing this and that. I cleaned the kitchen and bathroom, folded some clothes,and did a few more loads of laundry. I put together a supper for all of them that would be ready when the boys got home from school and daddy got home from work. When I got finished cleaning, George and I left. I hated leaving her like that. I didn't think she looked good at all.

The following morning, I told George that I needed to go to Nena's house. I just didn't like how she had been the day before. He agreed I should go. Even I hated to leave him alone, I had a feeling that I might not be back for a few days.

So off I go, praying all the way. Please God. Please God. George and Nena. Please God don't let them hurt.

I opened the door and walked right in to find my sister curled up in a ball on the couch. I go to her and wake her. She was slow to awaken. I had her sit up and open her shirt. At the site of the mastectomy was a hive about as big as a quarter. Nena didn't even know it was there. She was telling me that she was so nauseated all the time and had no energy. She had already gone through so much. All the surgeries, pin point radiation and chemo treatments. And here we are. Nowhere. Nena is losing this battle. In my eyes, not in hers. She never believed that this cancer would kill her.

After she finished telling me how she felt about the boys, the husband, the animals, and the house, I looked back at the hive. It had nearly doubled in size. I called the hospital and spoke directly to the doctor. He would be waiting for us and we should go straight to the ER. It would take one and a half hours. I got her dressed and really carried her to the car. Ninety minutes later, I had her in the emergency room. In the length of time it took us to get there, sister's hive had covered her chest and was starting up her neck. OH MY GOD! While the nurses were drawing blood, I took a minute to call our other sister to say I felt she needed to come. She agreed and would leave work immediately. I went back into the ER room and the rash was now all over her neck and in and all around her ears. Her chest was completely covered. She was sicker and sicker. They gave her something through the IV to calm her until the blood work came back. After she fell asleep, I went outside and called our brothers. I told them both that they needed to come and plan on staying for a while. She was so, so scared and about out of her mind with pain. The hive made it feel like she was trying to crawl out of her skin. The boys said yes and I felt relief they would be there. I called her husband, since I knew he'd be getting the boys off the bus. I told him we would all stay and that I would call him throughout the night. When I got back to her, she had just had another seizure. Now although she had been taking the seizure medicine for weeks already, it had been determined that she was having an allergic reaction to the seizure drug. They got her a private room and in came our other sister and our brothers. They were stunned when they seen Nena. She was so embarrassed and ashamed. We all just cried. Her skin had popped open like it was peeling. One week of around the clock care from the nursing staff and her siblings.

I'd call George every chance I got to tell him what all was going on. We all just felt so damn helpless. I'd go back and forth between George and Nena. We finally got to take her home, but for days and days afterwards, I would go to her house and redress the bandages, taking her to doctor's appointments and then more chemo treatments. After the cancer had spread to the brain and once they started with the whole head radiation, it was really the beginning of the end. Her body was no longer able to accept chemo or radiation, so they sent us home. She scheduled an appointment for the following week. She promised she'd have her counts back up by then. Truth be told, my sister didn't make it to that appointment. Instead, ten days later, after a beautiful dying, she passed away so peacefully at her home with her boys, her husband, and all of us siblings.

After all those days away from George, I couldn't wait to get home. It had started snowing earlier in the afternoon. By the time I got on the road, there were already three or four inches. I white-knuckled it all the way home.

When I did get there, George had hot soup on the stove, Sheba was in, and everybody was happy to see me. George looked pretty rough. He was so very sad about Nena. He loved her very much. He loved me too and was really proud. He could hardly even believe some of the stories during those days. I told him that his visit to see her meant the world to her. Whatever they spoke about was what she hung on to. He cried. Damn. George really did fall apart with Nena's passing. Losing his mother and his two sisters was enough, so this sent him right over the edge. His health really began to decline. Another funeral, another sister. OH MY GOD!

I had the family and the kids over as much as possible. We wanted them all to be a part of George's dying process. He wanted the children to be unafraid. The kids asked Uncle questions about it and he answered. We had to do it like this. Hard core lessons from a dying man. This man would be so missed. He couldn't just up and disappear from the kids. That would not work, at least not for this family. He shared the very end of his life with those he loved, and most of that time was with children.

George's breathing had become so very bad. Again I asked him about bringing oxygen in. This time he agreed. I called the doctor's office right then. I told them George was ready. The oxygen company called us within the hour. They would be at our house to set up in the early afternoon the same day. I readied the guest bedroom to put all the oxygen. I made lunch for us, then went into the bathroom after I finished eating. When I came out, George was gone. The oxygen people were to show up within the next half hour. He had run away from home.

Right on time, the lady showed up. I explained the situation. It didn't matter to her. She set him up anyway with anything he might need. We did put everything in the guest bedroom and shut the door. I listened to all the instructions and felt I had it down pat. I was to call her if I needed anything.

George came home a couple of hours later. There were no signs of oxygen in the living room and nothing was said between the two of us about it.

That evening, when he went to bed, he no more sooner laid down and he could not breathe. He was up and sitting on the edge of the bed. I sat next to him and politely asked if he cared to try some oxygen. He nodded his head. I went to the spare room and got the fifty foot hose, turned on the concentrator, and put oxygen on him. He sat for a few moments and then laid back down. He slept. I laid down alongside him listening for his breath. I had been doing this for months and months. Listening for how long it took from exhale to inhale. When I first started doing this, I would count to thirty. Months later, I was up to sixty. I would want to breath for him. I would want to shake him to breathe better. All I could do was count and pray. Pray I did. And count. It seemed as though he had gotten his best nights sleep with oxygen in a very long time.

In the morning when he got up, he admitted that using the oxygen was better. He used it most of that day, sitting in his recliner, Sheba laying next to him and watching the blizzard through our wonderful picture window. The only people on the road that day was the mailman and the milk truck driver. It was so nasty I didn't even want to go out and get the mail, but I did.

Father Bud called that day also to ask if he could visit the following day. George said yes but wasn't sure if the driveway would be plowed by then or not. It had really piled up with the wind just a blowing all day and all night.

Early the next morning, our neighbor was there with the big John Deere to dig us out. George stood at the window watching. I shoveled the front porch and sidewalk while Sheba ran around the yard playing in the deep snow.

I needed to get some groceries so when Father Bud came, I took my leave. The two of them had become friends since he had started coming for visits. It was very nice.

The holidays were upon us again. I was dreading them. George was not good. We were not able to go for Thanksgiving at my sister's house. My sister did send Thanksgiving dinner to us by way of a couple of the kids. After they left, they went and got the rest of the kids and brought them all to see Uncle. It did make him feel better. I know that when they left, they were crushed. It hurt them all. They could see Uncle failing.

Each day that followed, George was losing ground. I scheduled each family for visiting at Christmas, so as not to be so overwhelmed. Every child of each family spoke privately to Uncle as he laid in his recliner. Some of them even laid with him. Each told him, "I LOVE YOU UNCLE." I couldn't hear what any of them talked about or what he said to them. It wasn't for me to know. The kids needed to have this time with him. Understand that these kids are not toddlers anymore. They are now junior high and high school age. They know what's going on. For the last eight years we all watched George go through this. Oh hell, we all went through this. We went through it together. We'd gone through losing Nena and now George. Our kids were having to grow up and face tough issues. I didn't ever feel bad about this. I was very proud how we all dealt with my sister's disease, her dying process, and her death. I knew the children would take valuable lessons from their elders in what we did for her. The consistency of care we gave her would not have been possible had it not been for the kids in each house pitching in to help out their parents while they were away. Honestly, these kids and in-laws are stand up.

Because there were so many people coming in and out, I decided to put blue lights on the small tree outside. George could see it from the living room window. He always had said that blue lights looked holy. I agreed. Doing it this way allowed room for guests to come, sit and visit.

Some days George could visit. Some days he only slept while the people visiting sat quietly and watched as he rested. I wasn't to sure he would make it through the holidays, but he did.

January seemed to start out very cold even for Wisconsin. And the snow just kept on coming. It seemed like every couple of days someone was plowing our driveway.

It was always a treat when Father Bud would stop in. But when he came the first part of January, he told us that he was going to be transferred to another parish soon. The congregation wouldn't be to happy to hear that news. He was a wonderful priest and did so much for everyone. He would be sadly missed.

With that news, George asked him to give him his last rights. Father Bud done exactly that for him. George had then received all his sacraments through the Catholic church, which had been extremely important to him.

Another couple of weeks went by. George on oxygen 24 hours a day now, but still having a hard time to breathe. We were able to start putting morphine drops in his nebulizer which helped a little.

George and I had a lot of talks during those weeks. Mostly he talked and I listened. He spoke softly now and would be in and out even during a sentence. A person had to listen closely to what he said.

He couldn't sleep lying down anymore. He did a lot better in his recliner. It was a couch with a recliner on each end. I sat with him all the time. And so did Sheba. I sat in the middle right next to him and Sheba on the end next to me.

All three of us slept on the couch one evening. I got up early and made coffee and let Sheba out.

George needed help to get up off the couch that morning. I got him stood up, but he was shaky. I got him to the bathroom door. He stood there in the doorway holding on to the door frame. He steadied himself and standing there he announced that he felt like his body was shutting down. OH MY GOD!

I knew he was right. I said nothing. Still hanging on to him, I got him sat down on the toilet. I let him have his privacy, but after some time, I asked if he needed me to help him. He did need me. He had sat there all that time without success. He had no strength in his legs, so when I went to help him up, I couldn't budge him. We tried again and again, but we could not move him. I called my brother. He closed his store and came right over. While he was getting George back to the recliner, I made a few more phone calls as I knew we were approaching the end.

My brother stayed for a while before he returned to reopen his store. George still feeling like he needed to pee, but couldn't.

I called our hospice nurse and told her we needed a catheter. I knew he would hate it, but it needed done.

My brothers, their wives, my sister and her husband had all come over early that evening. George was so uncomfortable. All he could say is, "I got to pee." The nurse finally came when everyone was there. I had not told him that I'd called her. He thought this was just a surprise visit from her. After he told her what was happening with him then she put in the catheter. It was not pleasant.

The next couple of days George mostly slept. He didn't do any morphine or any of the rest of his pills. He didn't have any appetite.

My brothers and sister came every evening after work. The third night when they were all there they made me lay down to get a nap. I really didn't want to, but I was exhausted. I kissed George goodnight. He was only breathing through his mouth as he had been all day. I told my brothers that the oxygen wasn't doing him any good so I shut down the concentrator.

I have not any idea how long it had been when my sister came in to wake me. When I went to the living room, there they all were crouched around George, their hands touching him. I went and knelt down putting my hands and head on him. A few moments passed by and George drew his last breath. I could feel his spirit leaving his body. OH MY GOD!

I felt so light and so up lifted. I stayed touching him while my siblings made a few calls to their families. Then my brothers got out the booze and poured shots for all of us.

We toasted to that man who had once brought so very much joy to each of us. And then we had another shot. With big ole tears running down my face, I had to call the funeral home director as I had already talked to him and he was aware of our situation. He would bring the coroner. I also made the call to hospice.

When the director arrived with the coroner, he and I went to the basement to discuss the arrangements, while the coroner conducted his business and removed the body.

I'd had plenty of time over the years to think about a spectacular send off for my husband, the man that had meant so much to so many.

I'd given the funeral director as much information as I could. There were people I needed to talk to before anything was final. I needed to go to the funeral home to pick out a casket suitable for George.

I made a call to a cousin of mine to tell him George had passed. I also wanted him to stop in because I needed to ask him a favor. He obliged me and was at my house within the hour. Once there I asked my cousin how he would feel about getting a couple teams of horses together. One team to carry George to his resting place and the other for carrying the pall bearers. He was overwhelmed and gladly would do it. He said he'd be honored.

I then went to the funeral home. As is protocol, the director went through everything with me. When he wanted to know how many limos, I said none. I told him, I would be using horses and wagons. When he took me in to look at caskets, there wasn't any suitable. I wanted only a pine box. Indeed they had one stored away. That was the one I accepted.

I called eight of the nephews to ask if they would carry Uncle. Each of them agreed. I was delighted. We had boys from both sides of the family.

That's how it worked when I asked for speakers. One from each side for Eulogy. My brother was one. The other, a nephew from Colorado.

The auxiliary from St. Thomas had already called to tell me not to worry about anything. They would take care of the meal after the services.

I wanted to include some of the kids in our neighborhood to be part of this also. I made a plan, then asked their parents for permission.

I chose the music and spoke to the organist and choir director. They agreed on all the songs.

The local bar was normally closed the day we chose for the services. As luck would have it, the owners agreed to open up for the family. The dining room would be where the meal would be served.

Although I'd had years to get myself ready for this, I just seemed dazed. I was handling it, but I didn't feel good or right. I was alone. Surrounded by friends, neighbors, and family, I still felt alone.

Once all the planning and arranging was done, people started coming to the house. Anyone coming from a distance were making reservations at nearby hotels.

I had called everyone I could think of, but I needed to let just one more family know. For that, I'd have to drive to their place. I excused myself from the visitors and got in the car.

George had made friends with an Amish family about 20 miles away from our house. He used to go there to buy eggs and fresh vegetables. Every time he'd go there, all the children would go running out to him for that special piece of hard candy. There were ten children all together. The older kids are who he'd buy the eggs and veggies from. In the summertime, they'd have a roadside stand at the end of their driveway. In the winter, they'd sell out of the basement. They were all adorable and were so polite.

I wasn't sure how the Amish dealt with death, but I felt the need to tell them. I knocked at the back door and the children's mother answered. There she stood with her precious three week old baby in her arms. That made eleven children. I explained the reason for my visit. I could tell how sadden she was by this news. I felt better that I went there.

I had so many people in and out of the house. The Chicago family came with Italian sausage. One of the nephews and his wife began cooking. There was lots of family to feed. After they'd made their famous sausage and artichoke dish, then I took over the kitchen again. I wanted to have food for after the services at the bar. I made sausage, tomatoes, peppers, and onions for sandwiches. This was traditional Italian food for such an occasion.

People were driving and flying in from all over the country. I stayed busy trying to accommodate everyone.

It had been bitter cold for days. The neighbors had plowed the snow deep in the yard, so as to make room for people to pull in and park.

It was a party. Everyone was sad, but everyone was also happy. It was great to see both families getting together again and enjoying each other's company, in spite of the circumstances. They all knew that George could not be here forever and were relieved for him that he was out of pain and agony, and also knowing that a party would be exactly what George would have wanted.

The evening of the wake was so cold. It was minus ten degrees and the wind was howling, blowing drifts from the last snow storm.

I arrived at the funeral home and just sat in my car trying to get myself composed. I didn't know if it would be a good crowd or not because of the weather.

Finally, I walked in to view George's body. He looked so dapper in his black pin-striped suit. The pine box he laid in was adorned with flowers and his Stetson hat. OH MY GOD.

There were flower arrangements everywhere. The break room had been filled with food that my sister-in-laws had made. The receiving book was ready for the guests to sign. Someone had made a card box.

The families began to arrive. I wanted my siblings to be in the receiving line with me. Once we all lined up, it was non-stop for the next four hours. People, people, people. OH MY GOD.

The line of people went on forever. Groups of kids came together without their parents. The parents came separately. Coyote hunters and their wives came together. Parents with their children. George's doctor was there. It seemed like the weather wasn't going to stop any one. And then I look and there standing in the line was the Amish family. The parents, six of the children and the infant. OH MY GOD. To even think that these folks with a tiny baby would venture 20 miles in a one horse drawn buggy to attend this wake was remarkable. These are the kind of friends my George had made.

I was so glad my brothers and sister were there with me. I had been talking so much that I'd become hoarse. They really took over greeting for me. I got all the hugs and kisses. We had over 600 signatures in the receiving book. That's a lot of hugging, kissing, crying and talking.

I suppose I slept that night. I don't really recall. There was so much on my mind. Before day light, I'd had enough of tossing and turning. I put the coffee on and sat with a cup looking out that beautiful picture window. The yard light shining on all those vehicles parked in the yard. Sheba didn't know where she was supposed to be. She was curled up in a corner somewhere out of everybody's way since everyone started coming. Now in the quiet was just her and me. As the sun started to come up, I could tell it would at least be a sunny day, although cold and windy. I took advantage of the only bathroom and got ready for the funeral before anyone else got up.

I made a big breakfast for everybody. I was glad I had people in the house. It made what I had to go through on that day easier. I wasn't looking forward to anything that was ahead for the day. I needed to keep remembering that every single person was sad and also grieving for George.

I arrived at St. Thomas Catholic Church to find the two teams of Percheron horses hooked up to two different wagons. The one wagon already carried George's coffin. The horses had been groomed as if they were going to a parade. The pall bearers and others had gathered around the teams of horses and were talking about the route to take to the cemetery. I had chosen eight pall bearers. Two of the nephews were to ride with Uncle and the other six nephews had their own wagon to sit comfortably.

I went inside the church escorted by my brothers and took my place up front with the family. I stared straight ahead at the altar, now even more glorified by all the arrangements people had sent in remembrance. I heard the music begin and a sweet angelical voice from the choir singing, "The Old Rugged Cross". OH MY GOD.

The congregation stood as the pallbearers delivered the coffin to the alter. Children carried the chalice, candles and wine. The Priest followed. Once they had all reached the alter, my sister, nieces, and sister-in-laws draped the pall over the coffin.

The Father began with the greeting and opening prayer, followed by the first and second reading. He had chosen the Gospel according to Matthew 11: 25–30. His homily was received well.

The choir began with the offertory hymn, "How Beautiful", as children presented the gifts of bread, water, wine and purificator to Father. A rose and a red fern were then laid upon the coffin by the kids.

The red fern represented a book and a movie named "Where the Red Fern Grows". It was a movie George and I shared with the kids and a few of the parents over the years. It was about hound puppies, about dying, and about the red fern.

The mass proceeded as usual, the Lord's Prayer and the Sign of Peace. The choir sang "In the Garden" as everyone took communion.

My brother who was given the shirt right off George's back, rose from the front pew and took his place at the podium for the

Eulogy. He looked so handsome and so manly as he gazed out at his audience. He said all the following words:

"What is in a name?
   GEORGE (it is of Greek Origin)
   Known as 'Creator of a Fortune'
   A man who wanted for nothing but for others to be happy. He touched many lives. Always treating the little ones with his funny little stories and anecdotes. With a bibbed pocket full of hard candy, he could make the shyest child bold, the teariest child dry, and the smallest child tall. He shared with the children a taste for the finer qualities in life like 'anchovies and celery', how to make their cheeks all cherry red, and sharing the rake during 'leaf and pine needle harvest'.
   Our family was blessed with George as a family member 25 years ago. He was a loving husband to my sister, Nancy. His devotion to their relationship was a bond held strong. The values of family were landmarked for him. He brought to us the gift of his family.
   A gifted uncomplicated, sharing man, George gave of his talents much through his work. When the concrete trucks rolled in, stand back and watch the magic. Concrete was his passion, like clay to a sculptor. 'Don't forget to oil the forms!' he'd say.
   With his friends, George had many adventures. He learned of the hunt for coyote, deer, squirrels, and rabbits. He found solitude on the lakes and rivers. With the roll of the dice many of us will remember those 'happy fingers' and 'woofka woofka'. Campfires brought music and song to us all with his accordion cradled on his lap. 'Oh Solo—mio....' George brighten many a day for his special girls ages 8 to 80 with a flower and a note that read 'Just because you are you.' He was quite the baker's friend as I can vouch for and so can many others. Cream filled bismarks, apple fritters, jelly filled donuts, and a warm morning smile. He would say 'I must go now, my wife needs me.'

In the water, George was an anchor. On the water, he was a ship. With his true love of fishing, came stories of laughter and joy. The joy of sharing and most importantly, who got the quarter with the blue dot on it. Whiskers and fins filled scores of coolers and put on smiles of thanks in all who shared his catch. He has found a better place to fish and is watching over us all.

What is in a name, George? Creator of a fortune.

A fortune of family, of friends, a brother, a fortune maker.

You are God's temple and the spirit of God is living within you.

Goodbye our friend, goodbye our brother. Rest in peace."

Every single word my brother spoke was absolutely right on. Now I really was numb. I'd been holding it all together from the beginning. Those words grabbed me. Tears streaming down my face from the first sentence.

My nephew on George's side of the family took the podium and began his tribute to his Uncle George. That too was sad, happy and about how much he would be missed. Again very tearful for me. Everyone could feel the love this nephew had with his uncle.

"The Song of Farewell" was being sung by that angelical voice with the choir in the background. The funeral home director took off the fern and the rose. He handed it to the family and then took off the pall. Father then did the incense. The pallbearers took their place at the coffin as the choir began to sing "Amazing Grace." The boys placed the coffin in the wagon. Two boys stayed with Uncle's wagon and the other six loaded into the second wagon. The horses and the drivers had waited patiently. The lead wagon began the procession to the cemetery.

Two horse-drawn wagons being pulled by Percherons. My brothers and sister and me behind the last wagon. The congregation following behind. We all walked the distance from the church to the grave about six country blocks. It was very cold and windy, but still the sun was shining. I was feeling so proud and overwhelmed. What a beautiful send off. OH MY GOD.

I Listened For His Breath

The nephews, our boys, carried their Uncle George to his final resting place with tears in all eyes. Father anointed the coffin and gave the final prayer. I sat there. So did my brothers and sister. Much to our surprise, the crowd was lining up single file and walking past paying their respects. Each one laid a piece of hard candy on top of the coffin as they said their goodbye. It was unbelievable to me. Someone had thought up this idea. I was wowed by it all. I was the last to leave.

A friend had driven there and said he'd give me a ride back down to the bar where the funeral dinner was. The truck was good and warm as I was freezing. We had been outside for quite some time. I was glad we did it all just the way we did. So very beautiful.

A relative (who could afford it) gave the bar keep $500 and asked him to start pouring. And so the celebration of a life well lived and a life well loved began. Drinking, smoking, and telling tales at the bar. In the dining room, the auxiliary of the church was serving. Everyone raved over the food. When all had been fed and the dining room had cleared, we all pitched in to help with the cleanup and dishes. The bar was raising hell. The owner set the juke box to play without money for the night. The music constantly played. Every person was having a ball. Laughing, talking, eating Italian sausages, and dancing. Perhaps a dance on the bar. Right, sister?

I had so many of them tell me this was the best funeral they'd ever been to. That's a compliment. I felt the same way. I heard stories from different ones that I hadn't even heard before. More of George's kindness and family loyalty.

I took my leave, alone, early and drove to George's grave. I cried. Once I got home, Sheba and I had about an hour of silence. I went to bed shortly after everybody got back.

The following morning, anyone that had stayed in hotels, came by to say goodbye. George had asked me weeks back to make a list of names and things he wanted some to have. Before anyone left I gave away treasures to those George had specified. All were very touched. I don't think any of them will ever forget Uncle George's generosity.

It was a couple of days before everyone left. I had things I needed to get done. I prepared a list and added to it as I thought of things.

The very first thing was to go to an Amish family that lived close in our neighborhood. They made and sold superior furniture. I had drawn out a design of a wooden cross I wanted to use as George's headstone. The gentle man agreed to make it. I was to stop back in a couple of weeks to pick it up. He would do everything, including the wood burning. It seemed to me the man was anxious to get started on his new project. He had never been asked to do any thing like this before.

Once the cross was finished, my brother and I took it to the grave. We dug the hole, stood up the cross, and added the concrete, making sure it was level on all sides. My brother picked up everything and headed for home.

I sat there admiring the wooden headstone I had decided on. It was handsome, just like the body of the man that lay beneath it.

Epilogue

I HAVE BEEN TRULY blessed in my life. I've surrounded myself with the most stand-up people I have ever known. I have also gotten to caregive some of them. I give you this true story from my heart. My words do not do justice to the relationships revealed to you in this book. I will hope that you find some questions and answers to subjects you may have long thought about, but have not done anything about yet. Life is oh so short. Enjoy every day like it was your last day on earth. Do your best to live in peace and harmony. Take advantage of all God's gifts that have been given to you. We had yesterday, we have today, and perhaps we will get to see tomorrow.

God Bless You,
Nancy Seriani

Author Bio

NANCY SERIANI BORN IN the early 1950s, is the eldest of six. She was raised in a small farming community in southwest Wisconsin. She always looked after her younger siblings as well as many neighborhood youngsters and babies. Once out on her own, in all her different lives as she grew up, she has been taking care of someone. Long-in-the-tooth now, she continues taking care of. Love follows all those who care. She has much love in her life still. Nancy's life is quieter these days. She enjoys her gardens, her neighbors, friends and Jackson. Her yard is her sanctuary. It induces peace and joy. She no longer sits in a fishing boat. She now sits on a Harley Davidson.

Dedication

I DEDICATE THIS BOOK to those dying and to those who are caring for the dying. Either way, this is not easy. But if we can, we should try to get this done with as much dignity as possible, for those dying and those caring for the dying. For those dying; if you can, remember your caregiver is your everything, and will most likely be the one who is with you as you draw your last breath. Be grateful as you can that you have someone. For those caring for the dying, remember that could be you one day. How would you want to be treated? Are you doing all you can do to make the atmosphere nice for your dying loved one? More and more in these days of extremely high costs for skilled care and nursing homes, families are taking care of their own. Friends are taking care of friends. Neighbors are looking out for neighbors.

There's an old saying that goes something like this…WHAT GOES AROUND COMES AROUND…

Try to get as much gusto out of every day that you can.

GOD BLESS YOU ALL,
NANCY

Acknowledgements

GENERALLY THIS IS NOT how this is supposed to go, but, I would like to acknowledge myself. I started to write a love story many years ago. Now, it is sixteen years later. I have a T O T A L L Y different life now with another wonderful man. It hasn't been easy writing a love story about one man while sleeping with another. I am very proud to have finished. It is an honor for me to give you this true story about a very special man.

THANK YOU to Alma, my friend and mentor.

THANK YOU to Jackson and Craig.

A very special thanks to Charles H. Pabst, World renowned artist, and contributor to Leanin Tree who has allowed me to use one of his famous prints. I am honored to present this cover for "I Listened For His Breath".

THANK YOU Mr. and Mrs. Pabst.

Foreword

NANCY SERIANI IS A force of nature.

If you should find yourself or a loved one facing an unforgiving disease, you need a 'NANCY' on your team...someone protective, strong, loyal and loving.

Nancy has faced heartache and loss at the hands of cancer. Before, she told of the loss of her sister, Nena, in "FOR THE LOVE OF SISTER...a sibling's story". Now we gain a perspective of the loss of her husband, George.

Marches and Ribbons do not beat cancer. The best we can do is fight this disease to a "draw".

Your odds will improve greatly if you find a caregiver like Nancy. She has an iron glove over her velvet hand.

Craig Davis
2006 PBS TRANSPLANT SURVIVOR

A HEARTFELT *MÉMOIRE* OF devotion, commitment and compassion for her husband and the family members she cared for. A touching story.

DIANE J. HELM
AUTHOR 'FIRE ON THE WIND'

I HAD AN OPPORTUNITY to read Nancy Seriani's amazing book, "I LISTENED FOR HIS BREATH". Her beautiful rendition of her life with George touched my heart and brought tears to my eyes. Nancy says it best when she described "SPEAKING NO WORDS, WE TALKED THROUGH OUR HEARTS." She outlines their life together and at times, you can see her and George working side by side and making children [not their own] a part of their family.

I highly recommend Nancy's book to those who have been through the loss of a loved one, a partner, a soul mate. Nancy is truly inspirational.

REV. SUSAN HENLEY
AUTHOR, SPIRITUAL CONSELOR
"BECAUSE OF SEAN" the true story of a mother's courage.
"SARA, BEYOND THE VEIL" a spiritual look at dementia.

www.ingramcontent.com/pod-product-compliance
Lightning Source LLC
LaVergne TN
LVHW012126070526
838202LV00056B/5870